A Visit to New Jersey's Minor League Ballparks

Jason Love

Contents:

To Delia, Sophia and Ian

Introduction:

Tom Lohr wrote a book called *Gone to the Dogs.* Lohr visited every single Major League Baseball ballpark over the course of the season. He checked out several minor league parks as well. His goal was to rate the quality of the hot dog in each park. Lohr considered the ballpark's atmosphere, location, cleanliness and cost for the ticket and the hot dog. He did this on an extreme budget. His book was an inspiration.

Working full-time along with having three kids, I cannot afford to take a summer off to visit each ballpark across the country. However, I was inspired by Lohr's adventure. On a much smaller scale, I set out to watch each New Jersey professional baseball team play in 2019. I am a big baseball fan and figured this shouldn't be hard to accomplish. Living in South Jersey, I usually take in a few Phillies game each year. For full disclosure, I attended four of the five ballparks in New Jersey during the 2019 season. I went to Yogi Berra Stadium in 2017 but hopefully will get there to see the New Jersey Jackals play in the near future.

In 2008, Bob Golon's book *No Minor Accomplishment: The Revival of New Jersey Professional Baseball* focused on the return of professional baseball to the Garden State. It's incredible, but since his book the New Jersey baseball landscape has changed. The Newark Bears, Atlantic City Surf and the Camden Riversharks organizations have all folded. I had watched a few games at both Atlantic City and Camden and enjoyed their ballparks. For me, it was especially sad to see the Riversharks' Campbell's Field demolished in 2019. It was a great little ballpark tucked under the Ben Franklin Bridge. The ballpark had a grew view of the Philadelphia skyline. Campbell's Field was the only place I ever caught a foul ball at a professional baseball game. The stadium is now gone, but I still have the ball and some great memories of watching games there.

In many small towns, a minor league team becomes an important piece of the fabric which makes up the community. In her book *Minor League Baseball: Community Building Through Hometown Sports,* author Rebecca Krauss writes about how a minor league team often lifts the community spirit. Fans show true hometown pride in its team, players and ballpark.

Minor league baseball is not about glamour and high living. Ila Borders wrote about her experiences in her book *Making My Pitch*. Borders was one of the first female pioneers when it came to professional baseball. She played for the St. Paul Saints in the Northern League in 1997. In her book she talks about long bus rides, low pay and players hanging on to the dream of "getting the call." Teams such as the Somerset Patriots, New Jersey Jackals and the Sussex County Miners play in independent leagues.

The teams are not affiliated with a Major League Baseball team. The players are giving it one last shot or simply don't want to give up the game.

The movie *Bull Durham* starring Kevin Costner, Susan Sarandon and Tim Robbins was released during the summer of 1988. The movie proved to be a hit at the box office and will still run today on the MLB Network and other cable channels. It was nominated for Best Original Screenplay at the Academy Awards. Ron Shelton who wrote the screen play had played minor league baseball for five seasons. Shelton finally gave up the dream after the 1971 season never "getting the call."

Bull Durham really helped to revive interest in minor league baseball throughout the country. The film especially helped the Durham Bulls which saw a huge increase in fan interest in their team and ballpark. Around this time Mike Veeck took an interest in the Saint Paul Saints in the Northern League. Along with co-owners Bill

Murray (yes, the actor in *Stripes*) and Marv Goldklang, the three men purchased the team. Veeck brought a sense of fun to the ballpark and fans came out in droves. His unique sense of promotion and marketing was a great success. Around the country, minor league teams began to sprout up. New Jersey was no different. Baseball was returning to the Garden State.

In many ways, New Jersey residents have a chip on our shoulder. For those of us south of Trenton, we cheer for the Phillies. Everyone north of Trenton root for the Mets or Yankees. Sometimes it is annoying to live in the shadows of two major cities. We have our own identity. Heck, New Jersey has been home to Bruce Willis, Bruce Springsteen, Carl Lewis, Carlie Lloyd, Anthony Bourdain, Queen Latifah and Mike Trout. We gave the world *The Uncle Floyd Show* and *Weird NJ* magazine. New Jersey has its own identity AND personality.

Many people believe the game of baseball started in Cooperstown, New York. However, that has since proved to be more myth than fact. The first organized baseball game took place at Elysian Fields in Hoboken, New Jersey on June 19, 1846. The Knickerbocker Club of New York City faced off against the New York Nine. Alexander Cartwright was the official for the game. He came to be known as one of the first people to give the game some structure and established set of rules. Just for the record, the first game wasn't close as the Knickerbockers lost 23 – 1.

One of the most important minor league baseball games took place on April 18, 1946 when Jackie Robinson took the field in Jersey City at Roosevelt Stadium. More than 50,000 fans turned out to watch Robinson break the color barrier. Robinson was playing for the Montreal Royals which was the Brooklyn Dodgers top farm team. The Royals rolled over the Jersey City Giants 14 – 1 with Robinson collecting four hits including a home run. The following year Robinson would truly make history when he played for the Dodgers in what turned out to be a Hall of Fame career.

The Dodgers also have another connection to New Jersey. When Walter O'Malley was trying to get a new stadium built in Brooklyn, the Dodgers play a few games in Jersey City during the 1956 and 1957 seasons. O'Malley tried to use this as leverage as Ebbets Field needed serious upgrades. In the end the Dodgers moved to Los Angeles after the 1957 season. The baseball landscape was forever changed as the Giants followed in moving out west. New Jersey never did get a MLB team; however, minor league baseball is alive and well.

This small book provides an overview of each of the five organizations still playing baseball in New Jersey. Each team has its own unique features and identity. Most minor league ballparks provide a relatively inexpensive way for a family to take in a ballgame. Tickets fall in the

$10 - $15 range, parking is cheap and usually there is some type of giveaway or promotion. Although the level of play is not on par with Major League Baseball, any day spent at the ballpark is a good day. For me it is about sharing an experience at a baseball game with my son. Thank you for taking the time to read my book.

Enjoying a Minor League Ball Game

Chapter 1: Lakewood BlueClaws

If you are a Phillies fan, Lakewood is the place you want to visit to see rising stars or those players who are hoping to move up through the farm system. The BlueClaws were founded in 2001 as part of the Phillies organization. The team is one of their lowest level teams and play in the Class-A South Atlantic League. As of this writing, 90 players have gone through Lakewood on their way to play for a Major League Baseball team.

Lakewood is a unique town in New Jersey. It is home to a large Orthodox Jewish community. A lot of families have been moving into Lakewood from New York within the last several years. Many of the new residents are young families seeking cheaper real estate than what is available in Brooklyn. Lakewood has seen an incredible housing explosion in the last 20 years. In 2000 the town had about 60,000 people living in it. The population is now over 100,000 people. One interesting historic tidbit is Mookie Wilson lived in Lakewood for several years. Mookie is most famous for hitting a dribbler down the first base line in the 1986 World Series…

This area of New Jersey has a strong baseball connection. Nearby Toms River won the Little League World Series in 1998. This team featured Todd Frazier who started the championship game with a home run. Frazier has played with a few different Major League teams and is currently with the New York Mets. He still lives in Central New Jersey.

Al Leiter is from this area of New Jersey as well. Leiter had a long Major League Baseball career with several teams. He attended Central Regional High School in Bayville. He was drafted by the New York Yankees in the second round in 1984. Leiter was on the 1993 Toronto Blue Jays team that defeated the Phillies. His son Jack is an excellent high school pitcher. Leiter still lives in New Jersey with his wife and children.

The BlueClaws tapped into this positive baseball vibe in Central Jersey. In its first season in Lakewood, the team saw more than 480,000 fans watch them play at FirstEnergy Park. A young catcher named Carlos Ruiz caught 73 games for the team in 2001. This same catcher would later be part of Roy Halladay's no-hitter and perfect game. It is such an intimate ballpark. Fans really get a chance to see future stars up close and personal.

Like a lot of minor league parks, the BlueClaws offer post-game fireworks, promotions, giveaways and have a furry mascot. Lakewood's mascot is Buster and has been with the team since the team's debut in 2001. Buster attends every home game and even makes appearances outside the ballpark. As per his bio on the BlueClaws website, his favorite food is anything but shellfish.

FirstEnergy Park is set up with a "down the shore" type of theme. Fans can walk behind the outfield in an open concourse type area. The set up includes games that one would find on a boardwalk or carnival such as *throw a dart at a balloon*. Along the first base side is a small mini-golf course. The BlueClaws set up several large lifeguard stands where fans can sit and watch the game from the outfield. The ballpark has a grassy area directly behind the fence in left and right field where fans can stretch out, work on their tan, and watch some baseball. The concession stands sell freshly squeezed lemonade and funnel cake.

FirstEnergy Park was built in 2001 for $20 million and seats about 6,500 fans. It has 16 luxury boxes which can be rented out for birthday parties, corporate events or no special reason at all. The Township of Lakewood and the team initially agreed to a 20-year lease agreement. This lease was extended in the last few years to keep the

BlueClaws in Lakewood for a very long time. The team is currently owned by Art Martin and Shore Town Baseball.

Established in 1883, the Phillies have had minor league teams in several different cities throughout their history dating back to the 1930s. The Hazelton Mountaineers were their minor league affiliate from 1934 - 1936. The Mountaineers played in the New York-Pennsylvania League. The Spartanburg Phillies played in the Western Carolinas League for several years. Many future MLB Phillies played for Spartanburg including Larry Bowa and Manny Trillo.

One of the Phillies longest-running minor league teams is the Reading Fightin Phils. The team changed its name from the *Reading Phillies* to the *Fightin Phils* in 2012. The team has been playing in Reading as a Phillies farm team since 1967. Prior to becoming an affiliate with the Phillies, the team was part of the Red Sox organization.

Reading has a loyal fan base and currently play in
FirstEnergy Stadium.

The Phillies had their Triple-A team in Scranton-
Wilkes Barre for many years. From 1989 – 2006, the Red
Barons were the Phillies top minor league team. The
Scranton-Wilkes Barre team are now an affiliate of the
New York Yankees and changed their name to the
RailRiders. Many of the core members of the Phillies 2008
World Series team came through Scranton Wilkes-Barre
including Chase Utley, Ryan Howard and Cole Hamels.

Howard became the first member of the BlueClaws
to reach the majors. He made his debut with the Phillies
during the 2004 season. Plenty of Phillies have played in
Lakewood at least a short time during their baseball career.
Some alumni include Gavin Floyd, Carlos Ruiz, Randy
Wolf and J.A. Happ. In 2018 BlueClaws pitcher Spencer
Howard threw a no-hitter. Hopefully, fans will see him in
years to come pitching at Citizens Bank Park.

The BlueClaws create a very fan-friendly atmosphere to enjoy a game. The organization hosts many fun promotions throughout the season including *Elf* Night, *Star Wars* Night, Italian Heritage Night and Bruce Springsteen Appreciation Night. During the season kids can run the bases after the game on every Thursday, Friday, Saturday and Sunday. The team hosts several post-game fireworks nights as well. My favorite promotion was *Stranger Things* Night where the first 1,500 fans receive a *Stranger Things* fanny pack. What fan cannot use a fanny pack?

A ticket to see the BlueClaws is about $15.00 with a discount for seniors and children. Like most minor league ballparks, there is no bad seat in the stadium. The organization offers 5-game and 10-game membership plans. FirstEnergy Park has luxury suites which can be rented out for parties, outings or corporate events. The suites include 20 tickets, HD-television and indoor and outdoor seating. One unique feature with the BlueClaws are that select games features a concert *during* the game. The bands are usually some type of tribute group playing Grateful Dead or 80's music.

A game at Lakewood has a more chill vibe than the other ballparks. Maybe since it is only a short drive to Point Pleasant Beach and Seaside Heights, the ballpark has a relaxed atmosphere. FirstEnergy Park is a great ballpark. It is clean, the vendors are all friendly, and fans get a chance to see future Phillies stars (first round pick Mickey Moniak played in Lakewood during the 2017 season). It's not a bad way to spend a summer evening.

The game my son Ian and I attended was a perfect summer night. The fans were engaged throughout the game and knew quite a few of the players. One of the BlueClaws pitcher gave Ian a baseball after warming up between innings. It was a great night to enjoy a beer and a hot dog and a baseball game with my son.

Stadium Information: FirstEnergy Park 2 Stadium Way, Lakewood, NJ 08701

Ballpark Dimensions: 325'(Left), 325'(Right) and 400'(Center)

Affiliation: Philadelphia Phillies A-Affiliate

League: Class A South Atlantic League

Notable Players:

Cole Hamels was brilliant for the Phillies in the 2008 playoffs. He played a pivotal role in the Phillies winning their second World Series Championship. It's amazing, but Hamels has never won 20 games in a season. He made his debut with the Phillies in 2006 and soon became a central piece of the team's pitching staff.

Hamels played for the BlueClaws in 2003. During his time with Lakewood he went 6 -1 with an 0.84 ERA. Somehow Hamels is second only to George Rodriguez with the lowest ERA in Lakewood's history. Hamels' stay with the BlueClaws was brief as he quickly worked his way up through the Phillies farm system. Starting in 2007, he would win at least 10 games or more for six straight seasons. He was an All-Star with the Phillies three times.

Hamels became a fan favorite with the Phillies fans. Born in San Diego, he had a California cool about him but still connected with the fanbase. He and his wife Heidi were active in the community. They even donated their $9.4 million mansion in the Philadelphia area to charity after he was traded to the Texas Rangers. In his final start as a Phillies pitcher, Hamels threw a no-hitter against the Chicago Cubs.

Hamels had his number retired by the BlueClaws, and it is displayed along the outfield wall. The Phillies had the opportunity to bring Hamels back during the 2018 season as Texas was looking to trade him. Unfortunately, Philadelphia took a pass and Hamels ended up with the

Chicago Cubs. The Phillies could have used his arm as they quietly faded from the playoff picture during the final months of the 2018 season.

Ryan Howard hit 19 home runs and drove in 87 RBIs for the BlueClaws in 2002. During his stay in Lakewood he batted .280. Howard worked his way through the minor league system with only Jim Thome standing in his way. Eventually the Phillies traded Thome to make room for their young slugger. Howard would win Rookie of the Year for the Phillies in 2005 and the National League MVP in 2006. "The Big Piece" was one to watch at the plate with his power and massive home runs.

Born in St. Louis, Howard played college baseball for Missouri State University. He was inducted into the Missouri Sports Hall of Fame in 2019. The Phillies drafted Howard in the 5th round of the 2001 MLB Draft. He made his professional debut with the Batavia Muckdogs in 2001 before moving up to Lakewood the following year.

Howard eventually became one of the key players of the 2008 Phillies World Series team. He finished his career with 382 home runs for the Phillies. Unfortunately, his career was cut short due to injuries. The BlueClaws retired Howard's number 29 during the 2010 season. On July 14, 2019 the Phillies celebrated Howard at Citizens Bank Park. Dan Baker took the microphone to introduce Howard one last time to the sellout crowd who gave him a tremendous round of applause. Without "The Big Piece" the Phillies most likely would not have won the World Series in 2008.

Howard was similar to Thome in not only his power but in being one of the nicest players in baseball. During their time with the Phillies, neither one was never involved in any type of off-field controversy. Howard and his wife Krystle have founded the Big Piece Foundation which promotes literacy to children. The couple's *Little Rhino* books promote different positive messages to young readers.

Rhys Hoskins made his debut with the Phillies in 2017 and hit an incredible 18 home runs in just 50 games. He basically picked up where he left off in Reading and Lehigh Valley with the team's minor league organizations. He had hit 38 home runs for the Fightin Phils during the 2016 season.

Hoskins was drafted by the Phillies in the 5th round of the 2014 MLB Draft. He had played baseball for California State University. Hoskins played for the BlueClaws in 2015. In May of 2015 Hoskins was named Phillies Minor League Player of the Month. During the month of May he had batted .342 with two home runs and six doubles. He would not finish the season in Lakewood as he was promoted to the Clearwater Threshers before the year was up. Hoskins also played for the Australian Baseball League during the winter.

Hoskins also excels off the field. He is very involved in the Phillies' charities. He lost his mother to breast cancer when he was in high school. Her passing left a deep impression on him. Hoskins and his fiancé Jayme Bermudez volunteer their time to raise money for the Muscular Dystrophy Association. The couple hosted an MDA walk which raised money for the Philadelphia chapter of the non-profit organization.

Freddy Galvis was born in Punto Vijo, Venezuela and was on the radar of Phillies scouts while he was still a teenager. In 2004, he played for the Venezuelan team in the Junior League Baseball World Series. The Phillies signed him to a contract in 2006. Galvis made his debut with the BlueClaws in 2008.

Steve Jeltz was one of my favorite players when I was growing up. For some reason, Galvis was always one of my favorite Phillies players and reminded me of Jeltz. Maybe I have a soft spot in my heart for weak-hitting shortstops. Galvis was a great infielder. He made his Major League debut on Opening Day for the Phillies at second base in 2012. Chase Utley was hurt so Galvis was provided the opportunity to fill in. The Phillies won 1- 0 behind the pitching of Roy Halladay with Jonathan Papelbon picking up the save. That seems like a lifetime ago.

Galvis became the Phillies regular shortstop in 2015 while batting .263 with seven home runs. I have include Galvis among the notable players as I always liked his love of the game and his enthusiasm. In 2017 he played in all 162 games for the Phillies and then did the same the next year for the San Diego Padres. Although he is not a great hitter, he has excellent glove and is fun to watch. He currently plays for the Toronto Blue Jays.

Welcome to FirstEnergy Park

Close to the Action

Sunny Skies at FirstEnergy Park

Warming Up Between Innings

Here Comes Buster!

Play a Round of Mini-Golf Between Innings

Thanks to Ismael Cabrera who Gave my Son a Baseball

Chapter 2: New Jersey Jackals

"When you come to a fork in the road, take it," said Yogi Berra once while giving directions to a friend. Located on the campus of Montclair State University, the New Jersey Jackals play at Yogi Berra Stadium. Berra was a longtime resident of New Jersey and raised his family in the Montclair area. It is a bit off the beaten path, but it is a beautiful museum/ballpark combination. The Jackals are an independent minor league team playing in the Can-Am League.

The initial Can-Am League was started in 1936 with teams in upstate New York and Ontario, Canada. During WW II the league ceased operations as a lot of minor leagues suffered the same fate. With so many young men going overseas to serve in the military, there was a shortage of players for baseball. The Can-Am League started up again in 2005 as an independent league. The teams currently competing are primarily the following: New Jersey Jackals, Sussex County Miners, Rockland Boulders, Ottawa Champions, Trois-Rivieres Aigles and the Quebec Capitales. Teams will also play non-traditional minor league teams such as the Cuba National Team. Although baseball is known as America's Pastime, the Capitales have won the Can-Am Championship in 2006, 2009 – 2013 and 2017. Baseball is alive and well in Quebec!

The ballplayers in the Can-Am League truly play for the love of the game. Players earn about $2,000 - $3,000 per month and often live with host families in the area. In 2019 the owners in the Can-Am League discussed expansion plans into new markets in the Northeast. The teams currently play a 95-game schedule. The commissioner is Miles Wolff who has been involved with baseball for more than 40 years. Wolff began his career in professional baseball as the general manager of the Atlanta Braves AA-team in 1971.

In addition to being home to the Jackals, Yogi Berra Stadium hosts numerous other events throughout the year. In 2019 the ballpark held a Summer Food Truck and Craft Beer Festival. Fans could enjoy various microbrews along with live music. In July 2019 the Cycle Circus played three shows at Yogi Berra Stadium. Unlike a traditional circus with clowns and elephants, this show featured motorcycle riders doing stunts as well as riding in the Globe of Death. Seeing is believing! The Yogi Berra Museum also hosts baseball camps for youngsters between the ages of 7 – 13 during the summer.

Yogi Berra Stadium was built in 1998 and can accommodate approximately 5,000 fans if including the lawn seating. The money to construct the stadium was donated by Floyd Hall. He was a chief executive officer for Kmart from 1995 -2001. Floyd Hall Enterprises also built the ice arena for Montclair State University which also opened in 1998. The Floyd Hall Arena is just a short walk from the Yogi Berra Stadium.

Visiting the Yogi Berra Museum & Learning Center is a must if going to see a Jackals game. It is literally connected to Yogi Berra Stadium. Although Berra is often known for his funny sayings or "Yogisms" as they are known, he was one heck of a ballplayer. Not only was he a great catcher and hitter, Berra also collected a World Series ring for each finger and thumb. He was an 18x All-Star and won the American League MVP three times.

The museum is well worth the $10.00 admission charge. It is much more than just Yogi Berra uniforms and collectables. It is filled with different memorabilia mostly from the New York Yankees or the Mets. There is a small auditorium located in the museum which hosts various speakers throughout the year. In 2019 David Cone visited to talk about his new book. If you are a fan of baseball history, it is well worth a visit.

Tickets for the Jackals are affordable and parking is free. The prices for tickets range from $12.00 - $17.00 (Premium Field Box seats). On Sundays children 12 years and younger can get tickets for $5.00 for reserved seating. Like a lot of the minor league clubs, the Jackals offer various promotions throughout the season. Fans can purchase $1.00 beers on *Thirsty Thursday* nights along with a $2.00 hot dog. During the 2019 season, a fireworks display took place after every Saturday evening home game.

One of the interesting things about the Jackals' location is that they play on a college campus. Montclair State University is located just 12 miles from New York City. At some spots on campus, one can view the NYC skyline. It is one of the larger universities in New Jersey with more than 20,000 undergraduate and graduate students. Poet Allen Ginsberg briefly attended the college before transferring to Columbia University. Montclair State was founded in 1908 and is situated on 252 acres. In addition to the Jackals, the university's baseball team plays at Yogi Berra Stadium.

Since their inception, the Jackals have won more games than they have lost. The last few years have been a little rough, but they are usually a competitive team. The team routinely makes the playoffs and have won four championships. In their very first season the Jackals won the Northeast League Championship. In 2018 the Jackals averaged about 1,700 fans per game.

A visit to Yogi Berra Stadium is a nice daytrip. I would recommend visiting the museum as well as checking out the Jackals. If you enjoy baseball history, the museum usually has exhibits that cover many different eras of the game. There is enough to see and do for an afternoon spent on the campus of Montclair State University.

Stadium Information: Yogi Berra Stadium, 8 Yogi Berra Drive, Little Falls, NJ 07424

Ballpark Dimensions: 308'(Left), 308'(Right) and 398'(Center) – all end in 8 in honor of Berra.

Affiliation: Independent

League: Canadian American Association of Professional Baseball

Notable Players:

Pete Rose, Jr. had to follow in the footsteps of one of the greatest baseball players in the history of the game. His father is baseball's all-time leader in hits and a 17x All-Star. Rose, Jr. played in a total of 11 games for the Cincinnati Reds in 1997. The rest of his career was spent bouncing around the minors for several organizations. He also managed the Wichita Wingnuts for two season. During his tenure, the Wingnuts were a minor league team playing in the American Association of Independent Professional Baseball.

Rose, Jr. played for the Jackals in 1998 and 1998. He played well for the team during his time at Yogi Berra

Stadium. Looking at his career, the *Hit King's* son has a well-travelled journey in baseball. His first year in the minors was with the Erie Orioles in 1989. He has played for teams such as Winnipeg Goldeyes, Chattanooga Lookouts, Joliet JackHammers, Long Island Ducks, Lincoln Saltdogs, Newark Bears and Hickory Crawdads. He even spent time in the Mexican League with the Aguascalientes Rieleros in 2003. His final year of professional baseball was in 2009 with the York Revolution.

Did the younger Rose get a fair shot in professional baseball? It is hard to say because expectations were probably so high. One can only imagine the pressure he faced as being the son of such a high profile player. Sons of famous players have found success in Major League Baseball. Rose, Jr. was different though as his father faced so much controversy with the gambling and ban from Major League Baseball.

Raul Valdes was born in Havana, Cuba and has played baseball for the Jackals, Chunichi Dragons, New York Mets, St. Louis Cardinals, New York Yankees. Philadelphia Phillies and the Houston Astros. He even pitched in the Mexican League. Valdes has an interesting back story as he initially defected from Cuba while playing for the Cuban National team in 2003.

After leaving Cuba, he initially signed with the Chicago Cubs organizations. I would imagine the transition was difficult as he struggled to find his way with the Cubs. Valdes made his Major League Baseball debut with the New York Mets in 2010. Along with the Mets, he also pitched for the St. Louis Cardinals, New York Yankees, the Phillies for two seasons and the Houston Astros in 2014. Valdes pitched for the Jackals in 2006 and put up respectable numbers. He went 7 – 3 with a 2.81 ERA. He also had pitched for the Nashua Pride. As of this writing Valdes is still pitching professional in the Mexican League.

At 41 years of age, he is not quite ready to give up the game.

Johnny Hellweg played two seasons for the Jackals. He made 36 appearances as a relief pitcher in 2017. He earned a spot on the Can-Am League All-Star Team in 2017. Major League Baseball will usually scout players in the independent leagues. Hellweg's excellent play with the Jackals caught the eye of the Pirates. Pittsburgh bought his contract and sent Hellweg to their AA-team in Altoona, Pennsylvania.

Born in Ann Arbor, Michigan, Hellweg was drafted by the Los Angeles Angels in 2008. He was part of a trade that involved Zack Grienke and ended up with the Milwaukee Brewers. Hellweg made his MLB debut with the Brewers in 2013. After 2013, he bounced around the minor leagues for a few years.

Hellweg made it to the Pirates' AAA-team in 2018 but did not get called up. He finished the season with the Hiroshima Toyo Carp. He returned to play baseball with the Carp in 2019. Hellweg's journey in baseball has taken him around the globe.

Ed Ott was a coach for the New Jersey Jackals for several seasons. He is probably better known as a member of the Pittsburgh Pirates who had one of the shortest names in baseball. Ott was born in Muncy, Pennsylvania and drafted by the Pirates in 1970. He was part of the 1979 World Series team. His last season as a player was with the California Angels in 1981.

In addition to work with the Jackals organization, Ott also was a coach for the Houston Astros and Detroit Tigers. In 2015 the Jackals had a retirement ceremony for Ott at Yogi Berra Stadium. The team retired his number "14" which is displayed along the outfield wall. If you search out his name on YouTube, there is a great video of

Ott giving thanks to the fans on his special night.

Yogi Berra Stadium

Yogi Berra Museum & Learning Center

Derek Jeter and Yogi Berra Display

Yogi Berra: A Life Remembered

Welcome to Yogi Berra Stadium

Chapter 3: Somerset Patriots

The Somerset Patriots have found success with independent baseball where other franchises in New Jersey could not. The Patriots began play in 1998 in the Atlantic League. Due to construction delays, the Patriots played its first season on the road. In 1999 Somerset was finally able to call TD Bank Ballpark home. The team won early and continues to field a winning team. Since its inception the Patriots have picked up six League Championships.

The Patriots are linked with one of the more colorful personalities in the history of the game. The greatest moustaches in baseball history include: Rollie Fingers, Goose Gossage and Sparky Lyle. One of those three just happened to manage the Patriots from 1998 – 2002. Lyle guided Somerset to more than 1,000 wins as their manager. Even though he stepped down as their manager after the 2002 season, he still serves as a sort of goodwill ambassador for the team. Lyle's book *The Bronx Zoo* details his time spent with the New York Yankees. He pitched for several teams over the course of his Major League Baseball career including the Philadelphia Phillies, Boston Red Sox Texan Rangers, Chicago White Sox in addition to the Yankees.

The Patriots current manager is Brett Jodie. He served as the pitching coach for the team during Lyle's time as manager. Jodie has been with the organization for more than 15 seasons. He initially joined the team as a pitcher in 2003. He earned a 12 – 5 record during his first season with the team. Jodie briefly pitched for the New York Yankees and San Diego Padres during the 2001 season.

In 2019 Jodie reached a significant baseball milestone as he earned his 500th win as manager of the Patriots. To put it in perspective, Charlie Manuel had 1000th wins as manager of the Cleveland Indians and

Philadelphia Phillies over 12 seasons. Jodie credited Lyle for preparing him as a manager. It will be interesting to see if Jodie stays as manager of the Patriots or if he will move on to a ballclub affiliated with Major League Baseball in some capacity.

Like a lot of minor league teams, the Patriots host a slew of different promotions to bring fans to the park. In 2019 the team invited WWE Hall of Fame wrestler "Hacksaw" Jim Duggan for an appearance in July. Duggan was known for carrying his 2 x 4 piece of lumber and screaming "Hoooo" to the crowd. Fans could meet the 80s wrestling legend on the concourse during the game. Inviting wrestlers to minor league games is a popular promotion. During the 2019 season the Wilmington Blue Rocks invited Jake "The Snake" Roberts to a game for an appearance. What is more American than baseball and professional wrestling?

One of the more remarkable plays in baseball took place at TD Bank Ballpark during the 2019 season. The team's broadcaster Mark Schwartz caught a foul ball in the booth while calling the game. He actually called the play in which the ball sailed into the booth. The video of the play would go viral. It was a funny, surreal scene as he described the action. "I make the catch on the foul ball. I am very proud of myself," Schwartz said of the play. It is worth checking out on YouTube.

Some of the other promotions the Patriots have held is *Spongebob Squarepants 20th* Anniversary Night, Fortnite Night, *STAR WARS* Night and Bark in the Park. Actor Corbin Bernsen was also invited to make an appearance. Bernsen is most remembered for playing Roger Dorn in the movie *Major League.* Like all minor league teams the Patriots have fireworks after several games throughout the season. Throughout the game, kids are invited onto the field for various activities. The game I attended was an 11 a.m. game so plenty of kids from summer camps were in attendance. Despite the heat, Sparkee the mascot was working the crowd.

The Patriots are one of the more successful minor league teams in independent baseball. Their ballpark can accommodate 6,100 fans. Somerset routinely draws more than 5,000 fans per game which is excellent for a minor league team. The ballpark features a Party Deck as well as luxury suites.

The Patriots are owned by Steve Kalafer. He is also the owner of Flemington Car & Truck Country dealerships. Kalafer is active in the community as are the Patriots. The team hosts a golf outing every year with money going towards the Special Olympics as well as the Somerset Patriots Children's Educational and Sportsmanship Foundation. Throughout the year, players and coaches visit area schools to talk about bullying and saying no to drugs and alcohol.

Tickets for the games fall in the range of $12.00 - $15.00 per game. The Patriots also offer lawn seats for $10.00 available for purchase at the window. Parking is only $2.00 and right next to the ballpark. It looked like a lot of fans parked at the Target/Home Depot parking lot across the street for free. I didn't notice this until after the game. TD Bank Ballpark is easy to get to as it is near many main roads and highways. *Ballpark Digest* named it one of the best independent, minor league ballparks in 2015. My visit to see the Patriots was very enjoyable. I plan to return to the ballpark in the future to see more games.

Stadium Information: TD Bank Ballpark, 1 Patriots Park, Bridgewater, NJ 08807

Dimensions: 317'(Left), 315'(Right) and 402'(Center)

Affiliation: Independent

League: Atlantic League of Professional Baseball

Notable Players:

Tyler Cloyd's baseball career that has taken him not only around the United States but also around the globe. Drafted by the Phillies in the 18th round in 2008, Cloyd made it to the big leagues in 2012. He played two seasons with the Phillies before moving on to the Cleveland Indians organization.

Cloyd has bounced around with a few different organizations. In 2015 he signed a deal to play Korea Baseball Organization (KBO). His stint with the Patriots took place in 2017 where he pitched in a handful of starts. His contract was bought by the Mariners. He has also spent time with the Miami Marlins and Tampa Bay Rays but with little success. In 2019 Cloyd signed a deal with the

Mariners to play for the Tacoma Rainiers. This is his second time around with the Mariners' organization.

Nate Roe has never reached Major League Baseball, but he continues to be a favorite with the Somerset Patriots fan base. Roe is from Plainfield, New Jersey and played baseball for the Scarlet Knights of Rutgers University. His baseball career has provided him the opportunity to travel as he pitched briefly for the Adelaide Bite of the Australian Baseball League in 2016.

In addition to pitching for the Patriots, Roe has pitched for the New Britain Bees. He made the Atlantic League All-Star Game with New Britain in 2017. He has pitched for Somerset in 2018 and 2019.

Tim Raines was one of the most dynamic baseball players during the 1980s. He had tremendous speed and consistently hit above .300 during his career. He made his Major League Baseball debut in 1979, but people really took notice of him in 1981 as he made the All-Star team. He ranks as one of the greatest players to ever wear a Montreal Expos uniform. Raines also is known for his addiction to cocaine which nearly derailed his baseball career.

Elected to the Baseball Hall of Fame in 2017, Raines is probably the biggest star to have played for Somerset. He only played a handful of games for the Patriots, but he helped raise the level of respectability for the Patriots. Raines played for the Patriots in an attempt to showcase his talents to make the U.S.A. Olympics baseball team. Unfortunately, Raines did not make the Olympic team as they went with an extra pitcher instead. Raines batted .346 in playing seven games for the Patriots during the 2000 season.

Raines last played Major League Baseball in 2002 with the Florida Marlins. His remarkable career spanned four decades. He won three World Series rings and was a

7x All-Star. He also stole 808 bases over the course of his

career. The switch-hitting Raines was one of the best

leadoff men throughout the 1980s and 1990s. He retired

with 2,605 hits and a lifetime .294 batting average.

Baseball at TD Bank Ballpark

Sparkee Working the Crowd

Donald Trump Once Attended a Patriots Game

Marc Schwartz in Action

Entrance to the Ballpark

Somerset Patriots Championships

Chapter 4: Sussex County Miners

Baseball in Sussex County originally started out with a team affiliated with the St. Louis Cardinals organization. Skylands Stadium opened in 1994 with the New Jersey Cardinals taking the field. The Cardinals remained in North Jersey until the 2005 season. After the 2005 season, the team relocated to Pennsylvania near Beaver Stadium, home of Penn State football. The Cardinals became the State Spikes.

A newly formed Sussex Skyhawks team took the place of the Cardinals in Skylands Stadium. The Skyhawks played in New Jersey starting in the 2006 season. Due to financial difficulties the team folded after the 2010 season. The team never really established a fanbase and averaged less than 2,000 fans in their final season.

The Sussex County Miners were formed in 2015 and took the place of the Skyhawks. The team's name paid tribute to the area's history in zinc and iron mining. The Miners play in the Can-Am Association of Professional Baseball league. The team named David Chase as their general manager. Chase brought more than 30 years of baseball experience to the team. He left the team though after the 2016 season. Their current president of baseball operations is Greg Lockard.

Skylands Stadium located in Frankford Township is in the far northwest part of New Jersey. It is close to both the borders of Pennsylvania and New York. The township's population is approximately 5,500 people. Frankford Township is 35 square miles and has several unincorporated communities such as Augusta, Culvers Inlet, Culvers Lake and Wykertown. In addition to the ballpark, the Sussex County Fairgrounds are also located within the township's boundaries.

This area of New Jersey is known as the Skylands Region and features the highest point in the state. At 1,803 feet it is not exactly Mt. Kilimanjaro, but it is considered

high elevation for the Garden State. This region also

features 72 miles of the Appalachian Trail. This area almost

doesn't feel like New Jersey. From the top part of the

stands, one can see rolling green hills in all directions. It is

a different feel than all the other ballparks in New Jersey.

The Miners have one of the most unique mascots

and logo in all of baseball. Their mascot appears to be a

relative of Yukon Cornelius from the classic Christmas

special *Rudolph the Red-Nosed Reindeer*. Herbie the Miner

makes an appearance at every game at Skylands Stadium.

He's not quite the Phillie Phanatic, but the fans seem to

enjoy him. He strolls the concourse with his giant head and

bulging muscles greeting young fans. The ballpark ushers

all wear yellow miner helmets keeping with the mining

vibe.

Despite their mascot and beautiful, intimate

ballpark, the Miners struggle with attendance. In 2018 the

team drew 74,827 fans for the season. In 2015 the team only brought in 56,988 fans for their first season. This averaged out to 1,187 fans per game at Skylands Stadium. The team was still building its own identity. The game I attended with my son had a crowd of less than 1,000 fans. Despite the sparse crowd, the fans at the ballgame were very festive and vocal in their support of the team. After the game, fans were invited onto the field for autographs from the players.

Different events are held throughout the year to bring people to Skylands Stadium Skylands Stadiums features a Christmas Light Show and Village every year around the holidays. In addition to the light show, other events include beer festivals, food trucks and an Outdoor Recreation and Sportsmen's Expo. In 2019 Billy Ray Cyrus played a concert at the ballpark. Some other shows included the Nerds, Cycle Circus Stunt Show and the Drum Corps International.

During the summer the Miners host baseball camps for kids. Players and coaches teach baseball skills to children ranging in ages from 5 – 14 years of age. Adjacent to the ballpark is a 17,000 square foot sports training facility. Champions Way Sports Academy offers indoor batting cages and synthetic fields for various sports. It is not just a baseball academy but open to other sports as well.

The Miners had some historic moments during the 2019 season. On June 13 Frank Duncan threw the second no-hitter in the club's history against the New Jersey Jackals at Yogi Berra Stadium. He only walked one batter and retired the last 24 batters. Duncan credited his catcher Troy Dixon with calling a great game. It was an efficient outing on the mound as Duncan threw only 89 pitches.

Skylands Stadium can seat 4,200 fans with tickets in the $10.00 - $15.00 range. In such an intimate ballpark, there is not a bad seat in the entire ballpark. It features 10 luxury suites that can be rented out for games. Along the first base side is an open area with picnic tables under a large canopy. The third base side along the concourse also features a few tables with umbrellas. The food prices are reasonable. The team hosts different deals throughout the season such as Thirsty Thursday ($1.00 beers) and Waggy Wednesdays (buy one hot dog get one free).

The food options at the ballpark are not as plentiful as Citizens Bank Park or Citi Field. There is a concession stand serving the usual hot dogs and French fries. A nice touch is the server asks if you want sauerkraut with the hot dog. Skylands Stadium also features a stand with quite a few beer options besides the usual Coors Lite or Miller Lite. There is a small ice-cream shop where fans can get a good amount of ice-cream with toppings for $5.50. The wheelHouse Kitchen + Bar is located on site It offers a vast menu along with micro-beers and cocktails.

The ballpark was the longest drive from my home (Camden County area) but well worth the trip. The ballpark staff, people working the concession stands and even the players were all friendly. A visit to Skylands Stadium to watch the Sussex County Miners is a perfect way to spend a summer afternoon. My son and I were the only fans sitting along the third baseline when we went to the game. Three different players tossed baseballs our way. We did give one away to a kid sitting with her family along the concourse. It's always fun for a kid to leave the ballpark with a baseball souvenir.

Stadium Information: Skylands Stadium: 94 Championship Place, Augusta, NJ 07822

Dimensions: 330'(Left), 330'(Right) and 392'(Center)

Affiliation: Independent

League: Canadian American Association of Professional Baseball or the Can-Am League. Play 102-games from May through September.

Notable Players:

    Vic Black is a pitcher from Amarillo, Texas who was drafted by the Pittsburgh Pirates in 2009. He was drafted after playing at Dallas Baptist University. Black worked his way up through the Pirates organization before making his Major League debut with the Pirates in 2013. Pittsburgh traded him to the Mets in August of the same year. Black suffered a series of injuries that temporarily derailed his baseball career.

    Black signed with the Miners at the start of the 2017 season. His time in Sussex County was very brief as he then was signed by the San Francisco Giants organization a few weeks later. Black pitched for their Richmond Flying

Squirrels team and then the Salem-Keizer Volcanoes in Oregon. In 2018 Black was back in independent baseball playing for the New Jersey Jackals.

Kenny Koplove was born in Philadelphia, Pennsylvania and played baseball for William Penn Charter School. After playing for Duke University, he was drafted by the Phillies in 2015. His professional baseball career began with the Williamsport Crosscutters in the same year. He finished his first season with a 2 – 3 record and a 4.50 ERA. He split the 2016 season between Williamsport and the Lakewood Blue Claws. Koplove was picked up by the Miami Marlins and spent the 2017 with their minor league team Batavia Muckdogs.

Koplove joined the Miners in 2018 after spending time with both the Marlins and Philadelphia organizations. Over his career he has spent time both as a starting pitcher as well as coming in from the bullpen. After his lone season with the Miners, Koplove had his contract picked up by the

Colorado Rockies organization. He has spent parts of 2019 with two of their minor league teams: Albuquerque Isotopes and the Lancaster JetHawks (in California not Amish country in Pennsylvania).

Tyler Mondile was drafted in the sixth-round by the Cincinnati Reds in the 2016 Major League Baseball Draft. Mondile was a star pitcher for Gloucester Catholic High School in South Jersey. In a premier matchup, Mondile faced New Jersey's other top pitching prospect Jason Groome on May 16, 2016 in front of 6,000 fans. Mondile pitched a complete game as Gloucester Catholic won 1 – 0. Groome was later drafted by the Boston Red Sox in the first round of the 2016 MLB Draft.

Mondile spent some time with the Reds organization from 2016 – 2018. He was dismissed from their minor league team Dayton Dragons during the 2018 season while going 2 – 7 with a 6.51 ERA. Mondile returned to New Jersey and joined the Miners in 2019. In addition to the Reds organization, he also pitched briefly for the Washington Wild Things which in an independent team in Pennsylvania. Hopefully, his time spent in Sussex County will be a springboard to get back with an MLB team.

Bobby Jones is the current manager of the Sussex County Miners. Before leading the Miners, Jones spent time with several Major League teams. He should not be confused with former 76ers sixth man Bobby Jones of the same name. Jones (the baseball player) is a New Jersey native from Rutherford. He was selected by the Milwaukee Brewers in the 44th round of the 1991 Major League Baseball Draft.

Jones appeared in 99 games throughout his Major League career for four different teams. He pitched for the Colorado Rockies, New York Mets, San Diego Padres and the Boston Red Sox. He was a part of the 2000 Mets team that reached the World Series. In the National League

Divisional Series, he pitched a tremendous game at Shea Stadium against the San Francisco Giants. He pitched a complete game shutout and allowed only one hit. His win closed out the series and carried the Mets to the National League Championship Series. New York would go on to defeat the St. Louis Cardinals and go on to the World Series. Unfortunately, the Mets ended up losing to a strong New York Yankees team in the World Series.

Jones was hired by the Miners for the 2016 season. Prior to managing the Sussex County team, he was the pitching coach for the Rockland Boulders. The Miners job is his first opportunity at managing a team at the professional level. Since Sussex County won the 2018 Championship, it seems that Jones has been successful. He recently won his 200th game as the manager of the Miners.

Welcome to Skylands Stadium

A Perfect Blue Sky on a Sunday Afternoon

A Sunny Day for Baseball in Sussex County

Tyler Mondile Warming Up Before the Start of the Inning

The Friendliest Players in Baseball

Some Non-Baseball Fun for Younger Fans at the Ballpark

Rolling Green Hills Surround Skylands Stadium

Chapter 5: Trenton Thunder

"Trenton Makes – The World Takes" is boldly proclaimed on the Lower Trenton Bridge. At one time Trenton was home to many high paying jobs centered around manufacturing. The capital of New Jersey produced steel and iron which was exported to cities around the world. Like many industrial cities, these jobs eventually disappeared, and Trenton fell upon hard times. Trenton is the capital of New Jersey. During the week the city is busy with state workers in the downtown area. With the building of Mercer County Waterfront Park (now known as Arm & Hammer Park), the Trenton Thunder was a pivotal piece in the revitalization of the waterfront.

There was some debate as to where to build the ballpark for the team. Eventually it was decided to keep it within Trenton with the hope of bringing in additional businesses. Arm & Hammer Park is nestled along the

Delaware River. It is one of the few ballparks where a home run can possibly travel to another state. If the current is moving in the right direction, a baseball can clear the right field fence, land in the Delaware River and float across to Pennsylvania. Great American Ballpark in Cincinnati is located next to the Ohio River. It would need to be a monster home run though to clear the park, the Ohio River Scenic Byway, land in the Ohio River and then float across to Kentucky. To my knowledge, no player has hit such a home run.

Mercer County Waterfront Park opened in 1994 at an approximate cost of $16 million. There was a slight delay due to a severe winter which delayed construction costs. Thunder owner Joe Plumeri, Jr. added the name *Samuel J. Plumeri, Sr. Field* to the front of the ballpark as a tribute to his father. There is a statue of Samuel Plumeri sitting on a bench at the main entrance to the ballpark. Arm & Hammer eventually entered a licensing agreement with

the team hence the current name of the ballpark. Arm &
Hammer Park can accommodate 6,150 fans although it has
exceeded this on a few different occasions.

Of the five professional teams remaining in the
Garden State, the Trenton Thunder provide the highest
level of competition. The Thunder play in the Eastern
League which is at the Double-A level. Some of the other
teams include the Hartford Yard Goats, Binghamton
Rumble Ponies, Portland Sea Dogs and New Hampshire
Fisher Cats. Binghamton received some national attention
when Tim Tebow joined the team in 2018. On a visit to
New York a few years ago, I had the opportunity to visit
the Rumble Ponies' ballpark. NYSEG Stadium is a
beautiful, old-fashioned ballpark in its own right. If ever in
Binghamton, one should check out a game at the Mets'
minor league ballpark.

The Eastern League was actually founded in the
Arlington Hotel in Binghamton, New York in 1923. The

first game occurred on May 9, 1923 between Williamsport

and Wilkes-Barre. Since its inception, more than 50,000

Eastern League games have taken place. Some of the

alumni of the league include Mike Schmidt, Richie

Ashburn, Nolan Ryan and Greg Maddux. Hall of Famer

pitcher Robin Roberts actually finished his professional

career in the Eastern League in 1967. The 40-year old

Roberts pitched with the Reading Phillies before calling it a

career. Some current stars of Major League Baseball have

come through as well including Bryce Harper, Aaron Judge

and Manny Machado.

Trenton's population is going in the opposite

direction of Lakewood. New Jersey's capital reached its

peak in 1950 with approximately 128,000 people. With its

industry booming, jobs were plentiful. Since then the

population has been on the decline. By 1980 the population

had dipped below 100,000 people. Today about 85,000

people call the city home. Trenton is no longer in the top five among most populous cities in New Jersey.

Trenton previously had a minor league team for several years. The Trenton Giants were a minor league affiliate of a few different teams from 1946 – 1950. Their most famous player was Willie Mays who played for Trenton in 1950. Mays batted .353 for the Trenton Giants in the Interstate League. He made his debut with the New York Giants and 1951 and went on to be one of the greatest baseball players in history.

I live in South Jersey so I don't fully appreciate the pork roll. However, the Trenton Thunder have taken this food favorite to a whole new level. The classic pork roll sandwich at Arm & Hammer Park is quite delicious. In 2018 fans could purchase something called the *Sticky Pig* at Arm & Hammer Park. This healthy choice food included Case's pork roll, bacon, egg, cheese and a red pepper jam. All this squeezed onto a glazed donut. Personally, I'll stick to a hot dog with some mustard and relish. The ballpark also has a Chickie's & Pete's along the concourse of the first base side.

The food prices are reasonable at Arm & Hammer Park. I bought my children a bottle of water, French fries and a class pork roll sandwich for $10. On the concourse behind home plate is Killarney's on the Delaware which was serving up some local beers. I stuck with a Bud Light draft for $5.75 which isn't a bad price at a ballpark. Fridays are Pork Roll Fridays with fans being able to purchase a pork roll sandwich for just $2.00 throughout the 2019 season.

From pork rolls to dogs. A truly unique feature with the Thunder is the use of Bat Dog. The Thunder use a golden retriever as its Bad Dog for an inning or two during the game. Chase was the original dog for the Thunder and started in August 2002. Chase was followed by Derby keeping the job within the family. Rookie joined the

Thunder for the 2014 season and is now the third-generation member of the Bat Dog family. There is a great photo of Alex Rodriguez who was in Trenton for a rehabilitation start. A-Rod has a surprised look on his face while watching his bat being picked up by a dog. That's not something one sees at Yankee Stadium.

The Trenton Thunder are active in the community. The organization partners with non-profits such as the United Way and the Miracle League of Mercer County. The town also recognizes a Hometown Hero at each home game.

With tickets ranging from $12 - $15 there is not a bad seat at the ballpark. Kids and seniors only pay $11.00 for a ticket. Parking is only $5.00 and close to the ballpark. Arm & Hammer Park features a Fun Zone for children. Between watching Rookie retrieve the bats, quality baseball and a variety of food options, a visit to Trenton is well worth it.

Stadium Information: Arm & Hammer Park, One Thunder Road, Trenton, NJ 08611

Dimensions: 330'(Left), 330'(Right) and 407'(Center)

Affiliation: New York Yankees AA-Affiliate

League: Eastern League

Notable Players:

Nomar Garciaparra was a 6x All-Star and led the American League in batting average twice during his career. The Thunder were an affiliation of the Boston Red Sox when Garciaparra came through Trenton. He played for the Thunder during the 1995 season and batted .267 in 125 games. He made his debut with the Red Sox in 1996 for a few games. He was the American League Rookie of the Year in 1997. Garciaparra is a member of the Red Sox Hall of Fame. In addition to Boston, he also played for Chicago Cubs, Los Angeles Dodgers and the Oakland Athletics.

Garciaparra married soccer legend Mia Hamm in 2003. The couple have twin girls and a son. After retiring from baseball, Garciaparra worked for ESPN before joining the Dodgers broadcast team. He works alongside former MLB pitcher and one-time New Jersey resident Orel Hershiser. It's ironic that Garciaparra works in broadcasting considering he wasn't the most media-friendly person during his playing days.

George Case has a last name that is probably familiar to people in New Jersey who enjoy a pork roll sandwich. His father founded the Case's Pork Roll company in 1874. Case's pork products are still sold today throughout New Jersey, New York, Pennsylvania, Maryland and Connecticut.

George Case the ballplayer was born in Trenton in 1915. He was probably the fastest player of his era. Case led the league in stolen bases for five consecutive seasons. He played the bulk of his career with the Washington Senators from 1937 – 1947. He played for the Cleveland Indians for the 1946 season. Case was a 4x All-Star and probably had his best season in 1942 when he batted .320 with 44 stolen bases.

After retiring from Major League Baseball, Case's stayed involved with the game. He operated a sporting goods store in Trenton for several years. Rutgers University also had him as their baseball coach from 1950 – 1960. His son George III played for him for one season at Rutgers. He also served as a coach for several professional teams including the Hawaii Islanders, Washington Senators and was a scout for the New York Yankees, Texas Rangers and Seattle Mariners. Known for his sense of humility, Case passed away in 1989.

Derek Jeter/Roger Clemens/Alex Rodriguez all wore a Trenton Thunder uniform at one time during their careers. The greatest thing about affiliated minor league baseball is the fan gets to see rising stars or current stars who are injured and need a rehab game or two. Arm &

Hammer Park has hosted some games with some true superstars of the game.

Jeter made his rehab start with the Thunder in 2011. At the time of his visit to Trenton, the Yankees captain was 37 years old and just a few hits short of 3,000. Jeter traded his Yankees pinstripes for a stars and stripes uniform as the Thunder were celebrating the 4th of July. More than 9,200 fans came out to watch Jeter play at Arm & Hammer Park on July 3, 2011. More than 18,000 fans came out to watch Jeter play between the two games.

Clemens made his start for the Thunder during the 2007. The Rocket faced the Portland Sea Dogs. It is not often that a seven-time Cy Young winner suits up in a Trenton Thunder uniform. Clemens pitched before 9,134 fans on May 23, 2007. Clemens had initially broken the attendance record until Jeter's appearance.

A-Rod made his rehab start for the Trenton Thunder in 2013. Rodriguez hit a home run off pitcher Jesse Biddle of the Reading Fightin Phils. There is a great photo of Rodriguez with a bemused look on his face as the Thunder's Derby came out to retrieve his bat. It's not every day Rodriguez sees a dog work a ballgame in place of the bat boy. It is not confirmed if Jennifer Lopez visited Trenton to watch Rodriguez play for the Thunder…

Aaron Judge is probably the biggest star to play for the Trenton Thunder. At 6'7" and 275 pounds, Judge is built more like a linebacker than a baseball player. He was drafted in the first round by the New York Yankees in 2013 out of California State University – Fresno.

Judge quickly worked his way through the Yankees farm system. He played for Trenton during the 2015 season. In his debut at Arm & Hammer Park, Judge hit a walk-off home run in the 10th inning to lead the Thunder to a win over the Portland Sea Dogs. His home run cleared the

35' left field wall. The next year he played for Scranton Wilkes-Barre before getting called up by the Yankees.

David Eckstein has two World Series rings. He won one with the Anaheim Angels in 2002 and the other with the St. Louis Cardinals in 2006. He was the World Series MVP in 2006. Standing 5'6" tall, Eckstein did not look like your typical baseball player. He was drafted by the Boston Red Sox in 1997 and made his debut in Trenton in 1999. Eckstein did not make his Major League Baseball debut until 26 years of age. He would go on to play in the MLB for 10 years mostly with the Angels and the Cardinals.

The 5'7" Eckstein wrote a book called *Have Heart.* His book talks about the highs and lows of his career and the obstacles he overcame in becoming a professional baseball player. The book is part of the "Positively For Kids" series which is intended inspire children to reach their own goals. Eckstine retired after the 2010 season. He spent his last two years with the San Diego Padres.

Tom McCarthy never played for the Trenton Thunder but did work for the organization for six years. He was initially hired as director of the team's media relations in 1993. He worked both television and radio for the Thunder. McCarthy graduated from nearby Trenton State College (now The College of New Jersey) in 1990.

McCarthy worked for the Thunder up through the 1999 season. He left to join ESPN Radio 1680 AM. The Phillies hired him in 2001 for their radio broadcasts. After five seasons with the Phillies, he briefly worked with the Mets. McCarthy returned to Philadelphia for the 2008 season and has been with the team ever since. He currently works alongside either John Kruk or Ben Davis. Mike Schmidt and newest addition Jimmy Rollins will also work alongside McCarthy in the broadcast booth.

McCarthy is also an author and wrote a book *Baseball in Trenton* which focuses on the city's rich baseball tradition. He is in the Trenton Thunder Hall of Fame and still speaks fondly of his time with the Thunder. His oldest son Pat is following in his father's footsteps. Pat is the current play-by-play broadcaster for the Lehigh Valley IronPigs.

Arm & Hammer Park

Play Ball!

Everyone Enjoys a Pork Roll Sandwich!

Since 1870

Only in New Jersey is There a Pork Roll Mascot

Judge, Chase, Jeter and Severino Billboards

Trenton Thunder Bat Boy Tommy in Action

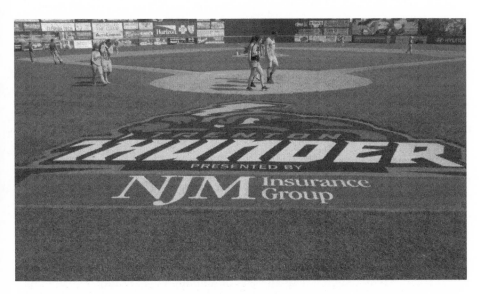

View from Behind Home Plate

The Delaware River Behind Arm & Hammer Park

Chapter 6: Past Ballparks and Ballclubs

The Atlantic City Surf, Newark Bears and Camden Riversharks all once called New Jersey home. These three teams all played in independent leagues and struggled to attract a steady fan base. The Bears came about from the vision of Rick Cerone who is a Newark native and played for the New York Yankees. The Riversharks were part of the revitalization of the Camden Waterfront. The Surf hoped to lure fans to Atlantic City who were looking for something else besides gambling in the casinos. Unfortunately, all three teams had some initial success but were not able to maintain it.

Of the three cities, Newark has the richest baseball history. The Newark Peppers played in the Federal League in 1915. The Federal League was a short-lived competitor of the National League and the American League that lasted two seasons. When the Indianapolis Hoosiers ran into financial trouble, the league moved the franchise to Newark. The Federal League wanted to tap into the New York City market.

The Peppers played in Harrison, New Jersey across the Passaic River from Newark. The Peppers played in Harrison Park which drew 30,000 fans on its opening day. Construction crews scrambled to get the ballpark ready for the home opener. The owner was Harry F. Sinclair. The team featured Hall of Fame player Edd Roush and finished with a record of 80 -72 in its lone season. The Federal League featured other stars of the day including Joe Tinker, Chief Bender and Cy Falkenberg (who played for both Indianapolis and Newark). Unfortunately, due to litigation, financial trouble and struggling franchises, the Federal League was not able to survive against the more powerful and established American League and National League. Newark would only have minor league teams after the Peppers franchise.

The Newark Bears that Cerone founded played from 1998 – 2013. The original Bears played in the International League from the 1920s up until 1949. The 1946 Bears team featured future Hall of Famer Yogi Berra. North Jersey also had the minor league affiliate of the New York Giants playing in Jersey City up until 1950. The most recent Bears played at Bears & Eagles Riverfront Stadium near the Passaic River.

When baseball returned to Newark in 1998 (technically, the team didn't play in Newark until 1999 as the ballpark wasn't ready) with the Bears, there was much talk if fans would come to support the team. Unfortunately, the team did not reach the expectations of ownership. Towards the end of their run, Riverfront Stadium had more empty seats than actual fans. The team had to file for bankruptcy in 2008 and eventually folder after the 2013 season.

Unlike Somerset, Trenton, Camden and even

Atlantic City, the Bears could not sell naming rights for the

stadium. It was simply known as *Bears & Eagles*

Riverfront Stadium. For a city with over 250,000 people, I

cannot figure out why the team could not come to terms

with a business to name the stadium. This would have

added extra revenue the team desperately needed to keep it

up and running. Also, I can imagine that it was a tough sell

to lure fans into Newark during the week or on weekends to

watch baseball. People from the suburbs always worry

about parking. The Bears played right in downtown

Newark so I can imagine parking was an issue for people

with young families coming to see a game.

The Newark Bears had a few highlights. The team

signed Jose Canseco in 2001. Signing with the Bears gave

Canseco a chance to play with his twin brother Ozzie. After

playing in a few games with Newark, the Chicago White

Sox took a chance on Jose and signed him as their DH to

finish the season. Ozzie hit 48 home runs for the Bears during the 2000 season.

Other MLB players in the decline of their career played for the Bears. Pete Incaviglia, Wes Chamberlain and Rickey Henderson also played for Newark. Former Pittsburgh Pirate great Bill Madlock even managed the Bears for two season. Cerone was able to use his Yankees ties to bring out legends such as Yogi Berra and Phil Rizzuto to make appearances at the ballpark. The team hosted various promotions throughout the season. Unfortunately, not enough fans came out to support the team in the end.

Jim Leyritz was given a second chance at baseball with the Newark Bears in 2011 when he was hired as the team's pitching coach. He played for several Major League teams during his career. Leyritz is probably most remembered for his time with the New York Yankees. He hit a clutch home run against the Atlanta Braves during the 1996 World Series.

Besides the Yankees, he played for the Anaheim Angels, Texas Rangers, Boston Red Sox, San Diego Padres and the Los Angeles Dodgers. He retired after the 2000 season. After his playing days were finished, he ran into some serious legal troubles. The former-catcher saw his hiring as the pitching coach of the Bears as a way to return to baseball and rebuild his life. Although he stayed for only one season in Newark, Leyritz remained involved with the game of baseball through a weekly radio show. He is actively involved in several charities including the PinkTie organization.

The magazine *Weird NJ* featured an interesting article on the ballpark in its May 2019 issue. The Bears hosted a Weird NJ Night during the 2007 season. The founders of the magazine – Mark Moran and Mark Sceurman – threw out the first pitch. The two Marks signed copies of their books along the concourse during this weird tribute night. For the 2019 *Weird NJ* issue of the magazine, Moran was invited back to take some photos of the ballpark. The ballpark is still standing currently, but it is hard to say for how long. I visited in July of 2019 but a chain link fence surrounds the ballpark.

Newark as a city has struggled over the years. It has seen something of a resurgence in recent years. It is home to both the New Jersey Performing Arts Center and the Newark Museum. The city has seen some national attention in the last few years. Cory Booker served as mayor from 2006 – 2013. His personality and high energy helped raise the profile of Newark. Booker's administration tried to reduce the crime rate and provide more affordable housing for its residents. He currently is a U.S. senator and is running for president.

Could a professional baseball team return to Newark? I would say it is highly improbable. Currently the

New Jersey Devils in the NHL play at the Prudential Center in Newark. The Devils had relocated from East Rutherford, New Jersey. The New Jersey Nets of the NBA left Newark in 2002 for Brooklyn, New York. In my opinion, baseball has a more difficult challenge to lure fans away from both the Yankees and the Mets.

Much like Newark, Camden is a city which had fallen upon hard times. The Camden Riversharks played their first game in 2001. Along with the aquarium and a concert venue, the Camden Waterfront was being built up. Campbell's Field was a beautiful ballpark with a great view of the Philadelphia skyline. With a professional baseball team, there was much talk about a great investment in the city. The Riversharks worked with the community to build up support and had a family-type atmosphere.

Campbell's Field was one of my favorite ballparks. When the Riversharks first came to Camden, my family and I would attend at least a few games each season.

Unfortunately, the team found itself struggling to stay afloat financially. One of the main issues with the Riversharks is that the Phillies played directly across the Delaware River. In addition to the Phillies, nearby minor league teams such as the Wilmington Blue Rocks and Trenton Thunder were affiliated with Major League Baseball.

Steve Schilling was a real estate investor who was the key figure in bringing baseball to Camden. A partnership was formed with Rutgers University-Camden and the City of Camden to have Campbell's Field built along the Delaware River. In the beginning fans did come to Camden to support the team. Tragically, Schilling died of brain cancer on May 7, 2003. His passing put the ownership of the Riversharks in jeopardy. The team continued on but would struggle to support itself financially in the years to come.

In its final years, the team offered many discounted and often free tickets to try and lure fans to Campbell's Field. In addition to the Riversharks, the Rutgers University-Camden baseball team would play its games at the ballpark. It was a great venue not just for baseball but for concerts as well. Bob Dylan even played a concert at Campbell's Field in 2005.

In 2015 the Riversharks made history by appointing Lindsay Rosenberg general manager of the team. She became just the second woman to be named general manager in the Atlantic League's history. Rosenberg worked her way up within the ball club by holding a variety of different jobs. She could often be seen walking the concourse before, during and after games lending a helping hand. Unfortunately, by the end of the season the Riversharks were not able to renew their lease at Campbell's Field.

Wilson Valdez is one former Major League Baseball player who suited up for the Riversharks. He played in Camden during the 2013 season after bouncing around with a few different MLB teams. Most Phillies fans will remember him coming in to pitch the 19th inning of a game against the Cincinnati Reds on May 25, 2011. The utility-player collected 270 hits over his career with a .236 batting average. His career pitching statistics are a 1-0 record with a 0.00 ERA. In addition to the Phillies, Valdez played for the Chicago White Sox, Seattle Mariners, San Diego Padres, Los Angeles Dodgers, New York Mets and finished up with the Reds. He even played in Japan and South Korea during his career.

The Riversharks also had some homegrown talent that played for its team. Brad Strauss from Haddon Township, New Jersey made Campbell's Field his second home. Strauss suited up for the Riversharks from 2001 – 2007. His best season in Camden came in 2003 when he batted. .331 for the season. Prior to joining the Riversharks, he also played professional baseball with the Long Island Ducks, Atlantic City Surf, Minot Mallards and the Zanesville Grays of the Frontier League. In 2017 Strauss was elected to the South Jersey Baseball Hall of Fame.

Another minor league team never took the place of the Riversharks. Due to its proximity to Philadelphia, the Phillies would have to have approved an affiliated minor league team. The Rutgers University-Camden baseball team played at Campbell's Field up until 2018. Campbell's Field was torn down in early 2019.

I have a special connection to the Atlantic City Surf. My friends took me to see the Surf for my bachelor party in 2001. Going to Cheerleaders or some type of gentleman's club wasn't my thing. Knowing I am a big baseball fan, we decided on seeing the Surf play and then headed to the Irish Pub for beers after the game. My friends like to joke that it was the lamest bachelor party in history, but I had a great time.

The Surf's first season was in 1998 playing at The Sandcastle. This was a great, little ballpark with a view of Atlantic City's casinos in the background. As the sun set, the lights of the casinos provided a wonderful backdrop. Atlantic City had a bit of history with professional baseball. The Bacharachs of the Negro Leagues played in Atlantic City for several years. One of the greatest players in Negro League history, Pop Lloyd, played for the Bacharachs. Lloyd was often compared to Honus Wagner. A nearby youth ballfield is named after Pop Lloyd.

As a team, the Surf found success in their first season. Atlantic City won the League Championship in 1998 by defeating the Bridgeport Bluefish. One of their first stars was Juan Thomas who hit 33 home runs in 1998. Thomas was a former prospect in the Chicago White Sox organization. The team was also able to sell the naming rights to their ballpark. It was renamed Bernie Robbins Stadium after a local jeweler.

The Surf like the Bears and the Riversharks were not affiliated with a Major League Baseball team. This always seems to hurt a minor league team. Independent teams do not have the luxury of future stars working their way up through the farm system. Teams rely on players who are looking for one last chance or former stars looking for a short-term arrangement to highlight their skills. The Surf never had much advertising help from the nearby Atlantic City casinos.

Mitch Williams was once hired to be the Surf's pitching coach. Before there was Kawhi Leonard, there was Joe Carter. Williams is probably best known for giving up the home run to Carter in the 1993 World Series. I always give Williams credit for not backing down from people asking him questions about the pitch. Not many pitching coaches though are known by the nickname "Wild Thing."

Williams had a decent career as a pitcher with several Major League Baseball teams. He fills in now doing commentary for 94.1 WIP on the morning show.

Jeff Ball batted .250 during his Major League Baseball career. He had one hit in four at-bats. He is currently an assistant coach with the Atlantic Cape Community College baseball team in Mays Landing, New Jersey. His career as a journeyman player has taken him to numerous cities/teams throughout the United States.

Born in California, he attended college at San Jose State University. The Houston Astros drafted Ball in the 12th round in the draft in 1990. His first taste of minor league baseball was with the Auburn Astros in the New York-Penn League. From there he played for the Osceola Astros in the Florida State League, the Jackson Generals, Quad City River Bandits, Tucson Toros, Phoenix Firebirds, Fresno Grizzlies before getting the call with the San Francisco Giants. His stay in the big leagues was brief. He went on to play for the Vancouver Canadians, Fresno Grizzlies again, and then joined the Newark Bears in the Atlantic League. He played briefly in the Mexican League before joining the Atlantic City Surf for the 2002 and 2003 seasons.

There has been talk of professional baseball returning to Atlantic City. The Atlantic-Cape Community College baseball team has been playing its games at The Sandcastle. The ballpark needs repairs such as plumbing, fixing the scoreboard and fixing the outfield fence. Atlantic City has been exploring the option of baseball again and even reached out to Frank Boulton. The city needs other options besides the casinos to lure families on the weekends. Boulton was a founding member of the Atlantic League and former owner of the Surf. He has the skillset and passion to bring baseball back to "America's Favorite Playground." Personally, I would love to see professional baseball played again in Atlantic City.

Most of the current minor league teams reside in North Jersey. Technically, Trenton and Lakewood are considered Central Jersey. I would love to see a minor league team return to South Jersey. Which city in the southern part of the state support a team? I don't have the answer to that question.

Entrance to The Sandcastle in Atlantic City

The Atlantic City Surf Once Played at this Ballpark

Entrance to Campbell's Field in Camden, New Jersey
(Photo from 2012)

Campbell's Field in the Process of Being Knocked Down
(2019)

Entrance to Campbell's Field (2019)

View of the Ben Franklin Bridge from Campbell's Field
(2007)

A Photo Through a Chainlink Fence

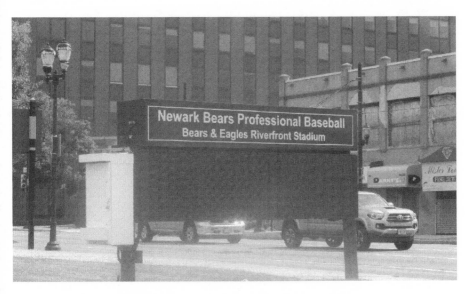

No Baseball Advertised These Days in Newark

Chapter 7: Negro League Baseball in New Jersey

This book would be incomplete without mentioning some of the Negro League teams that played baseball in New Jersey. Some great players also called New Jersey home including Larry Doby, Monte Irvin, Max Manning and Pop Lloyd. Across the Delaware River, several Negro League teams also played in Philadelphia. One of the most popular teams was the Philadelphia Stars who played in West Philadelphia throughout the 1930s and 1940s.

In 1920 Rube Foster met with other owners of black ballclubs in Kansas City to form the Negro National League. He set about providing league structure and a more regular season schedule for the Negro League teams. The Negro National League proved to be a success and provided stability not only for the teams but also the players. Foster was eventually elected to the Baseball Hall of Fame in 1981 for his contributions to the game.

One road trip I have to make one of these days is to the Negro Leagues Baseball Museum in Kansas City, Missouri. It's hard to imagine that baseball was segregated up until 1947. The museum initially opened in 1991 in a one-room office space. It moved to its much larger home in 1997 thanks to the championing of its cause by Buck O'Neil. His enthusiasm for the game of baseball is legendary. O'Neil's smile and positive attitude matched his love of baseball. One of my favorite books is *The Soul of Baseball: A Road Trip Through Buck O'Neil's* America by Joe Posnanski. It is well worth checking it out if you are a fan of baseball, history or both.

New Jersey had several successful black teams in the first half of the 20th Century. The Newark Eagles played in the Negro National League from the mid-1930s up until 1948. In addition to Irvin and Doby, some other feature players included Leon Day, Ray Dandridge and Biz Mackey. The Eagles played at Ruppert Stadium where the original Newark Bears also played their games. The ballpark was eventually demolished in the 1960s. The Eagles were owned by Effa Manley. She was the first woman elected to the Baseball Hall of Fame. One fascinating aspect of Manley is that she was critical of Branch Rickey of the Dodgers. She felt the Negro League teams should have been compensated for the players they lost to Major League Baseball.

One player who was never given the chance to play in the MLB is connected to Atlantic City. The Bacharach Giants in Atlantic City had one of the greatest shortstops to play the game of baseball in Pop Lloyd. Many baseball historians refer to Lloyd as the "black Honus Wagner." Over the course of his 27-year career, Lloyd played for several Negro League teams including the Philadelphia Giants, Hilldale Daisies and the Cuban X-Giants. It was in the twilight of his career when he played professionally in Atlantic City.

Lloyd was elected to the Baseball Hall of Fame in 1977. Sadly, he had passed away in 1964. He spent his final years working as a custodian in the Atlantic City school system. He was active in recreation baseball leagues and popular in the community. A youth baseball field in Atlantic City is named "Pop" Lloyd Stadium in his honor.

Another important figure in the history of baseball was Larry Doby who was born in Camden, South Carolina but moved to Paterson, New Jersey as a teenager. He played for the Newark Eagles. After returning from military service, he helped the team win the Negro National League World Series in 1946. One of his teammates with the Eagles was Monte Inrvin. Doby's level of play in Newark put him on the radar of Bill Veeck who eventually signed him to play for the Cleveland Indians.

Doby followed Jackie Robinson as being the second black player in Major League Baseball and the first in the American League. Doby made his debut with the Cleveland

Indians on July 5, 1947. He is often overlooked as helping to break down the color barrier in baseball. Everyone knows about Robinson and the racism he encountered while playing for the Brooklyn Dodgers. Doby faced the same adversity and treatment while playing for the Indians.

Doby primarily played for Cleveland but also saw action with the Chicago White Sox and Detroit Tigers. Doby was the first black ballplayer to hit a home run in the World Series. He was the second black manager in Major League Baseball (Frank Robinson was the first). Doby lived an amazing life that is often overshadowed by Jackie Robinson, Frank Robinson, Hank Aaron and Willie Mays. However, Doby was just as important in breaking down barriers. He also was one of the first Americans to play overseas in Japan. Upon retiring, he hit 253 home runs and had a .283 lifetime batting average. Doby was elected to the Baseball Hall of Fame in 1998. He died in Montclair, New Jersey in 2003.

As mentioned, Doby played with Monte Irvin who also has a connection to New Jersey. He was born in Alabama, but his family moved to Orange, New Jersey when he was a child. Irvin played for the Newark Eagles in 1938. After serving in the military during WW II, Irvin played for the New York Giants from 1949 – 1956. He made his Major League Baseball debut as at thirty years of age. Irvin won a World Series championship with the Giants in 1954 over the Cleveland Indians. He was elected to the Baseball Hall of Fame in 1973.

An important historical structure of the Negro League days is Hinchliffe Stadium. Nestled along the Passaic River, the stadium was built in 1932 for $350,000 in Paterson, New Jersey. The stadium became a popular venue for boxing matches, auto-racing, football games and concerts. The New York Black Yankees called Hinchliffe Stadium home for 12 seasons. In addition to the Black Yankees, the New York Cubans played there during the

1930s. It was at Hinchcliffe Stadium that Doby was discovered by the Newark Eagles in 1942.

In recent years a push has been made to save what is left of Hinchliffe Stadium. It is one of the few remaining structures still standing that has a link to Negro League Baseball. Once the original Yankee Stadium was torn down, it is the only one in the New Jersey/New York area. Sadly, a lot of the old ballparks that once fielded Negro League teams have been torn down. Hinchliffe Stadium is one remaining link to the glory days of the 1940s era of baseball.

A few years ago I had the opportunity to talk with Robert Scott who played for the New York Black Yankees in the 1940s. Scott was making an appearance at a baseball card and memorabilia convention in Wildwood, New Jersey. He was sitting at a table and selling photos along with his baseball card. As a baseball historian, it was fascinating to talk with someone who experienced segregated baseball firsthand.

Scott was playing baseball in Macon, Georgia when he was signed by the New York Black Yankees as a teenager. The pitcher spent several seasons for the Black Yankees. He told me his team played at Yankees Stadium in the Bronx in front of large crowds. He had the opportunity in the 1940s to play with Doby, Don Newcombe and Roy Campanella. His salary during his days in Negro League Baseball was only a few hundred dollars per month. In 2017 he was inducted into the Macon Sports Hall of Fame.

After he left baseball, he moved to New Jersey and worked as a bricklayer until retirement. I purchased a baseball card from him which he signed for me. He was gracious and did not seem to have any animosity about never being given the chance to play Major League

Baseball. It was obvious he had a love for baseball and simply enjoyed playing the game.

How would baseball be different if there was not segregation? Would Josh Gibson be ranked alongside Babe Ruth and Hank Aaron in home runs? How many wins would Satchel Paige have picked up if he started for the Cleveland Indians in 1928 rather than 1948? He probably would have won more than 400 games. It is fun to think about how different the game's history would be if the color barrier was never in place.

Pop Lloyd Stadium in Atlantic City

Scoreboard at Pop Lloyd Stadium

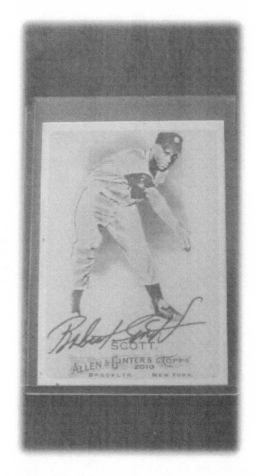

Autographed Robert Scott Baseball Card

Bibliography

Applebome, Peter (2010, May 24) Our towns: more is at stake than saving an old stadium in Paterson. *The New York Times*, p. A19.

Capezzuto, T. (1993, October 17) Professional baseball coming to Sussex county. *The New York Times*, p. 17.

Chase, M. (1998, March 4) Doby is named to Hall of Fame. *The New York Times*, p. A1.

Curry, J. (2001, April 20) Newark signs Jose Canseco. *The New York Times*, p. D6.

Curvin, R. *Inside Newark.* New Brunswick, New Jersey: Rutgers University Press.

Foster, F. *The Forgotten League: A History of Negro League Baseball.* Bookcaps (2012).

Golon, B. *No Minor Accomplishment: The Revival of New Jersey Professional Baseball.* New Brunswick, New Jersey: Rivergate Books (2008).

Garner, R. (1999) A new ballpark has some bullish, others bearish. *Business News New Jersey.* Vol. 12 (27) p. 7.

Greene, J. (2001) Pay no attention to his past. *Sports Illustrated.* Vol. 96 (26) p. R2.

Krauss, R. *Minor League Baseball: Community Building Through Hometown Sports.* Binghamton, New York: The Haworth Press (2003).

Moran, M. There used to be a Newark ballpark. *Weird NJ.* Vol. 52, pp. 26-33.

Okkonen, M. *The Federal League of 1914-1915*. Garrett Park, Maryland: The Society for American Baseball Research (1989).

Steele, A. (2015, September 4) Camden Riversharks may be leaving town. *Philadelphia Inquirer,* p. B04.

Thunder Road: Game Program. May 2019.

Ward, J. (2002). You build it, will they come? *American City & County*. April 2002, pp. 38-45.

Websites

https://ballparkdigest.com/

https://baseballhall.org/

https://www.baseball-reference.com

https://canamleague.com/

http://www.caseporkrollnj.com/

https://frankfordtownship.org/

http://friendsofhinchliffestadium.net

http://www.maconsportshof.com

https://www.milb.com

https://www.mlb.com/

https://nlbm.com/

https://sabr.org

http://southjerseyhotstovers.com/

http://www.thebaseballcube.com

https://www.timelessbaseball.com

http://www.trentonnj.org/

https://www.visitnj.org/regions/skylands

Team Websites

https://www.milb.com/lakewood

https://www.milb.com/trenton

http://njjackals.pointstreaksites.com/view/njjackals/

https://www.somersetpatriots.com/

http://sussexcountyminers.com/

About the Author

Jason Love was born in Camden, New Jersey. He works for Rutgers University and enjoys taking his children to baseball games throughout the summer. His lifetime batting average was .220 playing Little League baseball. He can be followed on Twitter @jason_love1.

Author's Little League Team (1982)

Made in the USA
Middletown, DE
06 February 2020